How to handle kids with Autism

Keys to parenting children with autism for successful parenting

Steve J. Dawson

table of content

Chapter 1

The reality about Kids with Autism.

What's It Like to Have Mental imbalance Range Issue?
A youngster with mental imbalance could experience difficulty:

talking and learning the significance of words
making companions or fitting in
managing changes (like difficult new food sources, having a substitute educator, or having toys moved from their typical spots)
managing clearly clamors, splendid lights, or groups
Kids additionally could move in a strange manner (like fluttering their hands) or do exactly the same thing again and again (like saying a similar word).

A youngster with mental imbalance might experience a little difficulty with these things, or a great deal. A few children need just a smidgen of help, and others could require a ton of help with learning and doing ordinary stuff.

What Causes Chemical imbalance?
Mental imbalance is something individuals are brought into the world with. Nobody knows precisely exact thing aims it. It likely has something to do with a youngster's qualities and different things that meaningfully have an impact on the manner in which the cerebrum creates.

How Is Chemical imbalance Analyzed?
Specialists actually take a look at infants and young children for indications of mental imbalance at each exam. A parent might feel that something is off-base and tell the specialist. Perhaps the youngster

is mature enough to talk yet doesn't. Or on the other hand a youngster doesn't appear to be keen on individuals or plays in strange ways.

At the point when a specialist figures a youngster could have mental imbalance, the person in question will work with a group of specialists to check whether it is mental imbalance or something different.

How Is Mental imbalance Range Problem Treated?
There is no solution for mental imbalance, however treatment can have a major effect. The more youthful children are the point at which they start treatment, the better.

Specialists, advisors, and custom curriculum instructors can assist jokes around with figuring out how to talk, play, and learn. Specialists likewise assist messes with finding out about making companions, alternating, and getting along.

Imagine a scenario where My Companion Has Mental imbalance Range Problem. Certain individuals with ASD don't feel that they have an issue and don't have any desire to change. They're glad for what their identity is and they need to be acknowledged, despite the fact that they might have various qualities and shortcomings than most others.

All individuals merit regard. In any case, jokes with ASD might be prodded, tormented, or left out in light of the fact that they're unique. Harassing and prodding are never the correct method for treating others, yet it very well might be difficult to be a companion with somebody who has ASD.

Messes with ASD frequently don't grasp perky jokes. You might should be exceptionally clear when you speak with somebody who has ASD.

Attempt to be patient and kind. Recollect how hard it very well may be for the individual with ASD to comprehend how to be a companion. Defend cohorts who are tormented. Tell grown-ups, so they can assist with safeguarding kids who are harassed.

Chapter 2

What are the signs of Autism

.

Indications of ASD normally become obviously clear during youth, between ages 12 and two years. In any case, side effects may likewise show up prior or later.

Early side effects might remember an undeniable deferral for language or social turn of events.

The DSM-5 partitions side effects of ASD into two classifications:

issues with correspondence and social communication
limited or dull examples of conduct or exercises

To be determined to have chemical imbalance, an individual should encounter side effects in both of these classifications.

Issues with correspondence and social collaboration
ASD can include a scope of issues with correspondence, a large number of which show up before age 5.

Here is an overall timetable of what this could resemble:

From birth: inconvenience keeping in touch
By 9 months: not answering their name
By 9 months: not showing looks intelligent of their feelings (like shock or outrage)
By a year: not participating in fundamental intuitive games, similar to surprise or pat-a-cake

By a year: not utilizing (or just utilizing a couple) hand signals, similar to hand-waving

By 15 months: not imparting their inclinations to other people (by showing somebody a most loved toy, for instance)

By year and a half: not pointing or looking where others point

By two years: not seeing when others seem miserable or hurt

By 30 months: not participating in "imagine play," like really focusing on a child doll or playing with puppets

By 60 months old enough: not playing turn-taking games, similar to duck goose

Also, mentally unbalanced youngsters could experience difficulty communicating their sentiments or understanding those of others beginning at three years.

As they age, they could experience issues talking or extremely restricted talking abilities. Other medically introverted youngsters could foster language abilities at a lopsided speed. Assuming there's a specific point that is exceptionally fascinating to them, for instance, they could foster an extremely impressive jargon for discussing that one subject. Be that as it may, they could experience issues conveying about different things.

As mentally unbalanced kids start talking, they could likewise talk in a surprising tone that can go from shrill and "sing-songy" to mechanical or level.

They could likewise give indications of hyperlexia, which includes perusing past what's generally anticipated of their age. Youngsters on the mental imbalance range could figure out how to peruse sooner than their neurotypical peers, some of the time as soon as age 2. In any case, they tend to not understand what they're perusing.

While hyperlexia doesn't necessarily in every case go with chemical imbalance, research recommends almost 84% of kids with hyperlexia are on the range.

As they collaborate with others, medically introverted kids could experience issues offering their feelings and interests to other people or find it hard to keep up with to and fro discussion. Nonverbal correspondence, such as keeping in touch or non-verbal communication, could likewise stay troublesome.

These difficulties with correspondence can persevere over the course of being an adult.

Confined or dull examples of conduct or exercises

Notwithstanding the correspondence and social issues referenced above, mental imbalance additionally incorporates side effects connected with body developments and ways of behaving.

These can include:

dreary developments, such as shaking, fluttering their arms, turning, or running this way and that

lining objects, as toys, up in severe request and lashing out when that request is upset

connection to relentless schedules, similar to those around sleep time or getting to school

rehashing words or expressions they hear somebody say again and again

flying off the handle over minor changes

zeroing in eagerly on pieces of items, similar to the wheel of a toy truck or the hair of a doll

uncommon responses to tactile info, similar to sounds, scents, and tastes

fanatical interests

uncommon capacities, similar to melodic ability or memory abilities

Different attributes

A few medically introverted individuals could encounter extra side effects, including:

postponed development, language, or mental abilities

seizures

gastrointestinal side effects, similar to clogging or loose bowels

inordinate concern or stress

uncommon degrees of dread (either higher or lower than anticipated)

hyperactive, negligent, or incautious ways of behaving

surprising close to home responses
surprising dietary patterns or inclinations
surprising rest designs

Indications of mental imbalance in small kids include:

not answering their name
keeping away from eye to eye connection
not grinning when you grin at them
lashing out in the event that they could do without a specific taste, smell or sound
dreary developments, like fluttering their hands, flicking their fingers or shaking their body
not talking as much as different youngsters
rehashing similar expressions
Chemical imbalance in more established youngsters

Indications of chemical imbalance in more established youngsters include:

not appearing to comprehend what others are thinking or feeling
finding it hard to say how they feel
loving a severe everyday daily practice and blowing up in the event that it changes
having an exceptionally distinct fascination with specific subjects or exercises
flying off the handle in the event that you request that they follow through with something
finding it hard to make companions or liking to be all alone
taking things in a real sense - for instance, they may not comprehend phrases like "break a leg"
Chemical imbalance in young ladies and young men

Chemical imbalance can in some cases be different in young ladies and young men

For instance, mentally unbalanced young ladies might be calmer, may conceal their sentiments and may seem to adapt better to social circumstances.

This implies chemical imbalance can be more earnestly to recognize in young ladies.

Chapter 3

Being a caring parent

Assisting Your Child with Autism Thrive There are numerous things you can do to assist a kid with Autism Spectrum Disorder (ASD) conquer their difficulties.

These nurturing tips, medicines, and administrations can help.

Closeup of kid wearing earphones

A parent's manual for chemical imbalance treatment and backing

Assuming you've as of late discovered that your kid has or could have chemical imbalance range jumble, you're most likely pondering and agonizing over what comes straightaway. No parent is at any point ready to hear that a kid is something besides cheerful and sound, and an ASD determination can especially terrify. You might be uncertain about how to best assistance your kid, or confounded by clashing treatment exhortation. Or on the other hand you might have been informed that ASD is a serious, long lasting condition, leaving you worried that nothing you really do will have an effect.

While the facts confirm that ASD isn't something an individual just "outgrows," there are numerous medicines that can assist youngsters with gaining new abilities and beat a wide assortment of formative difficulties. From free taxpayer supported organizations to in-home conduct treatment and school-based programs, help is accessible to meet your kid's unique necessities and assist them with learning, develop, and flourish throughout everyday life.

While you're caring for a mentally unbalanced kid, dealing with yourself is likewise significant. Being major areas of strength for genuinely you to be the best parent you can be to your kid out of luck. These nurturing tips can help by making existence with a mentally unbalanced kid more straightforward.

Try not to sit tight for a conclusion

Everything thing you can manage is to begin treatment immediately. Look for help when you suspect something's off-base. Try not to hold on to check whether your kid will look up some other time or grow out of the issue. Don't sit tight for an authority determination. The previous kids with chemical imbalance range jumble find support, the more noteworthy their opportunity of treatment achievement. Early mediation is the best method for accelerating your youngster's turn of events and diminish the side effects of chemical imbalance over the life expectancy.

At the point when your youngster has chemical imbalance
Find out about chemical imbalance. The more you are familiar chemical imbalance range jumble, the better prepared you'll be to go with informed choices for your kid. Teach yourself about

the treatment choices, get clarification on some pressing issues, and take part in all treatment choices.

Turn into a specialist on your kid. Sort out the thing triggers your child's difficult or problematic ways of behaving and what gets a positive reaction. What does your kid see as unpleasant or startling? Quieting? Awkward? Pleasant? Assuming you comprehend what influences your kid, you'll be better at investigating issues and forestalling or changing circumstances that cause challenges.

Acknowledge your youngster, eccentricities what not. As opposed to zeroing in on how your mentally unbalanced kid is unique in relation to different youngsters and what the person in question is "missing," practice acknowledgment. Partake in your child's unique idiosyncrasies, celebrate little triumphs, and quit contrasting your youngster with others. Feeling genuinely cherished and acknowledged will help your kid more than anything more.

Try not to surrender. It's difficult to foresee the course of mental imbalance range jumble. Try not to rush to make judgment calls about the thing life will resemble for your kid. Like every other person, individuals with mental imbalance have a whole lifetime to develop and foster their capacities.

Assisting your youngster with chemical imbalance flourish tip 1: Provide construction and wellbeing
Realizing all you can about chemical imbalance and engaging in treatment will go quite far toward aiding your kid. Moreover, the accompanying tips will make day to day home life simpler for both you and your kid with ASD:

Be steady. Kids with ASD struggle with applying what they've realized in one setting (like the specialist's office or school) to other people, including the home. For instance, your youngster might utilize gesture based communication at school to convey, yet never remember to do as such at home. Establishing consistency in your kid's current circumstance is the most ideal way to support learning. Figure out what your youngster's specialists are doing and proceed with their methods at home. Investigate the chance of having treatment occur in more than one spot to urge your kid to move what the person in question has gained starting with one climate then onto the next. It's likewise vital to be reliable in the manner you collaborate with your kid and manage testing ways of behaving.

Adhere to a timetable. Mentally unbalanced youngsters will more often than not do best when they have a profoundly organized timetable or schedule. Once more, this returns to the consistency the two of them need and long for. Set up a timetable for your youngster, with standard times for dinners, treatment, school, and sleep time. Attempt to downplay interruptions. Assuming there is an undeniable timetable change, set up your youngster for it ahead of time.

Reward acceptable conduct. Encouraging feedback can go quite far with kids with ASD, so try to "discover them accomplishing something great." Praise them when they act suitably or become familiar with another ability, being unmistakable about the thing conduct they're being applauded for. Likewise search for alternate ways of compensating them for good way of behaving, for example, giving them a sticker or allowing them to play with a most loved toy.

Make a home wellbeing zone. Cut out a confidential space in your home where your kid can unwind, have a solid sense of reassurance, and be protected. This will include putting together and defining limits in manners your youngster can comprehend. Obvious prompts can be useful (hued tape stamping regions that are untouchable, marking things in the house with pictures). You may likewise have to somewhere safe and secure proof the house, especially assuming your kid is inclined to fits of rage or other self-harmful ways of behaving.

Tip 2: Find nonverbal ways of interfacing Associating with a mentally unbalanced kid can be testing, yet you don't have to talk — or even touch — to impart and bond. You convey by the manner in which you take a gander at your kid, by your manner of speaking, your non-verbal communication - and perhaps the manner in which you contact your kid. Your kid is likewise speaking with you, regardless of whether the individual in question won't ever talk. You simply have to get familiar with the language.

Search for nonverbal signs. Assuming you are attentive and mindful, you can figure out how to get on the nonverbal signals that mentally unbalanced kids use to impart. Focus on the sorts of sounds they make, their looks, and the signals they use when they're drained, hungry, or need something.

Sort out the inspiration driving the fit. It's simply normal to feel upset when you are misjudged or disregarded, and it's the same for kids with ASD. At the point when youngsters with ASD showcase, it's frequently on the grounds that you're not getting on their nonverbal signs. Pitching a fit is their approach to imparting their dissatisfaction and certainly standing out.

Set aside a few minutes for entertainment only. A youngster adapting to ASD is as yet a kid. For both medically introverted youngsters and their folks, there should be something else to life besides treatment. Plan recess when your youngster is generally ready and conscious. Sort out ways of having some good times together by contemplating the things that make your youngster grin, giggle, and emerge from her/his shell. Your kid is probably going to partake in these exercises most on the off chance that they don't appear to be remedial or instructive. There are enormous advantages that outcome from your satisfaction in your kid's organization and from your kid's happiness regarding investing unpressured energy with you. Have is a fundamental impact of learning for all kids and shouldn't feel like work.

Focus on your kid's tactile awarenesses. Numerous kids with ASD are overly sensitive to light, sound, contact, taste, and smell. A few youngsters with chemical imbalance are "under-delicate" to tactile upgrades. Sort out what sights, sounds, scents, developments, and material sensations trigger your child's "terrible" or problematic ways of behaving and what gets a positive reaction. What does your kid see as upsetting? Quieting? Awkward? Agreeable? Assuming you comprehend what influences your kid, you'll be better at investigating issues, forestalling circumstances that cause challenges, and making effective encounters.

Tip 3: Create a customized mental imbalance treatment plan
With so many various medicines accessible, it very well may be hard to sort out which approach is ideal for your youngster. Making things more convoluted, you might hear unique or in any event, clashing suggestions from guardians, educators, and specialists.

While assembling a treatment plan for your youngster, remember that there is no single treatment that works for everybody. Every individual on the chemical imbalance range is exceptional, with various qualities and shortcomings.

Your kid's treatment ought to be custom fitted as indicated by their singular necessities. You realize your kid best, so it ultimately depends on you to ensure those necessities are being met. You can do that by posing yourself the accompanying inquiries:

What are my kid's assets - and their shortcomings?

What ways of behaving are creating the most issues? What significant abilities is my youngster lacking?

How does my youngster learn best - through seeing, tuning in, or doing?

What does my youngster appreciate - and how could those exercises be utilized in treatment and to support learning?

At long last, remember that regardless of what treatment plan is picked, your contribution is crucial to progress. You can assist your kid with seeking the most out of treatment by working connected at the hip with the treatment group and finishing the treatment at home. (Therefore your prosperity is fundamental!)

A decent treatment plan will:
Expand on your kid's advantages.
Offer an anticipated timetable.
Show errands as a progression of straightforward advances.
Effectively connect with your kid's consideration in exceptionally organized exercises.
Give normal support of conduct.
Include the guardians.
Picking chemical imbalance medicines
There are various choices and ways to deal with ASD treatment, including conduct treatment, discourse language treatment, exercise based recuperation, word related treatment, and nourishing treatment.

While you don't have to limit your child to just one treatment at a time, it's unlikely you'll be able to address everything at once. Instead, start by focusing on

Chapter 4

Listening to your kids and Handling your emotions

.My child is on the mental imbalance range and gets baffled when he have zero control over the discussion. He'll begin saying "enough" and moping. I've had a go at requesting that he lift his hand when he needs to talk. Yet, he gets baffled when I answer by requesting that he let the other individual completion. Whenever I offer him the chance to talk, frequently he simply makes something up or offers something that has neither rhyme nor reason. I've been not able to persuade him that we can advance by paying attention to individuals. Counsel appreciated.

two or three individuals posturing for the camera

The present "Got Questions?" reaction is by kid analysts Rebecca Hellenthal (left) and Megan Norris, of Nationwide Children's Hospital Child Development Center and Ohio State University. The clinic and college are among the 14 destinations in the Autism Speaks Autism Treatment Network.

Supervisor's note: The accompanying data isn't intended to analyze or treat and shouldn't replace individual interview, as fitting, with a certified medical care proficient as well as conduct specialist.

Much obliged to you for your inquiry. Many individuals impacted by mental imbalance experience issues dominating discussion abilities. This can demonstrate very disappointing, both for those on the range and their discussion accomplices.

This is an extraordinary subject to examine with your child's conduct specialist, language instructor or potentially custom curriculum educator. In a perfect world, you need to work with them to plan a customized help and learning program for your child.

In the interim, you can attempt a few methodologies at home. They follow the overall three-step approach we frequently use to address conduct difficulties:

Survey the issue (for example sort out the individual's challenges and assets)
Show new abilities in a strong manner
Practice these new abilities.
So you could begin by get-together data about what your child truly does well in a discussion and what is hard for him. For example:

Improves when a discussion focuses on one of his number one points, however shows little interest in different subjects?
Is it true or not that he is great at beginning discussions, however not standing by listening to somebody answer?
Does he take a gander at his discussion accomplice when he talks? When the other individual talks?
Does he answer on point when someone else asks his perspective or if make an effort not to draw in him in a conversation?

Having a rundown of qualities and regions for development can assist you with explaining the objectives you set for your child and give him the criticism he wants en route.

Rehearsing discussion abilities
For example, it seems like your child appreciates conversing with others. That is certainly a strength. Simultaneously, it seems like he experiences issues when he isn't the one talking. To work on his tuning in and answering abilities, have a go at rehearsing with a thoughtful third individual so you can assist your child with thinking of a remark or question about what the other individual said.

For instance:
Companion: "I just saw the new Avengers film."

You to your child: "What could you get some information about the film or his opinion on it?"

Make certain to laud your child's endeavors - both in posing an inquiry and afterward paying attention to the reaction. Simultaneously, have tolerance and make little strides that support achievement.

For example, consider provoking the discussion accomplice ahead of time to keep his reaction short before all else. Assuming your child effectively pays attention to the reaction, acclaim him. You could then urge him to answer, thus, by sharing something he ponders the film (on the off chance that he's seen it) or a connected film.

application, schedule

Notwithstanding acclaim, think about a prize framework. It could include a little treat or prize tokens on a board that he can trade out for a most loved movement or little toy. You realize best what will spur your child.

a nearby of a toy
Utilizing visual backings
Many individuals on the mental imbalance range work best with obvious prompts. There are a few supportive choices for showing conversational turn taking. One includes a "talking stick" that your child and his discussion accomplice pass to and fro to flag whose turn it is to talk. (See photograph above.)

a drawing of an animation character

On the other hand, you can print or draw "tune in" and "talk" signs, for example, those displayed at left. Hold up each obvious sign during your training discussion meetings to prompt your child when it's his move and when to pause and tune in.

Utilizing points and questions
One more fun method for rehearsing a scope of discussion abilities (turn-taking, seeking clarification on some pressing issues, expanding on others' viewpoints) is to record a few themes or inquiries on bits of paper that you place in a bowl. Model subjects could incorporate games, school and family. Model inquiries could incorporate "What is it that you need to be the point at which you grow up?" "What is your number one film?" "What is your #1 memory from when you were pretty much nothing?"

Alternate picking a piece of paper from a bowl and expressing something about its point or question.

Keep your turns short from the get go, so your child needs to tune in for just a brief time frame before you commendation or prize him. As he gets better at tuning in and holding up, attempt continuously protracting your responses (or those of another accomplice).

We like consolidating this game with the talking stick or tune in/talk signs.

Record and survey
One more technique that a few families find successful is to video record their youngster having a discussion with someone else. In a steady manner, watch the video together and discuss what worked out positively and what could be gotten to the next level.

This can assist you and your child with distinguishing extra regions for development -, for example, how to pose an explaining inquiry or fittingly end a discussion.

A significant number of the kids we work with incredibly appreciate seeing themselves on record.

A connected methodology is to watch a clasp of two individuals having a discussion in a film or network show. Then, at that point, discuss what they did and didn't get along nicely. We call this video displaying, and it could be particularly useful assuming your child appreciates screen time.

As usual, give a ton of commendation and positive consideration for your child's endeavors. Underscore his readiness to deal with these abilities instead of just "taking care of business." Remember to bring up things he gets along nicely - whether it's tuning in or holding on to represent even a couple of moments or making an on-point remark.